ASSASSINATION OF THE PRESIDENT.

A DISCOURSE

ON THE DEATH OF

ABRAHAM LINCOLN,

PRESIDENT OF THE UNITED STATES.

DELIVERED AT ACTON, MASS., APRIL 16TH, 1865.

REPEATED IN THE BAPTIST CHURCH, WEST ACTON, JUNE 1ST, 1865.

BY REV. GEO. W. COLMAN,

PASTOR CONGREGATIONAL CHURCH, ACTON.

BOSTON:
S. CHISM,—FRANKLIN PRINTING HOUSE,
NO. 112 CONGRESS STREET.
1865.

ASSASSINATION OF THE PRESIDENT.

A DISCOURSE

ON THE DEATH OF

ABRAHAM LINCOLN,

PRESIDENT OF THE UNITED STATES.

Delivered at Acton, Mass., April 16th, 1865.

Repeated in the Baptist Church, West Acton, June 1st, 1865.

BY REV. GEO. W. COLMAN,

PASTOR CONGREGATIONAL CHURCH, ACTON.

BOSTON:
S. CHISM,—FRANKLIN PRINTING HOUSE,
No. 112 Congress Street.
1865.

NOTE.—This discourse has been but slightly modified since its first delivery. What was then immediate and present is now past. The change of tense and the poem of Wm. Cullen Bryant are all that seemed necessary to adapt it to this day of National Humiliation and Prayer appointed by President Andrew Johnson.

SERMON.

. . . Know ye not that there is a Prince and a great man fallen this day? . . . The Lord shall reward the doer of evil according to his wickedness.—2 SAM. iii. 38, 39.

WHEN Massillon came to preach the funeral sermon of Louis the Fourteenth of France, he chose these words of Solomon, "I communed with mine own heart, saying, Lo, I have become great!"* And, slowly repeating them over, as if to recollect himself, "Lo, I have become great!" then fixing his eyes on the assembly in mourning; next surveying the funeral enclosure, with all its sombre pomp; and lastly, turning his eyes on the tomb erected in the midst of the cathedral,—after a solemn pause, he exclaimed, "God alone is GREAT, my brethren!" The immense assembly was breathless with solemnity and awe.

With such a thought as this, we come to the house of God to-day. Such an occurrence as that which we now lament was never before known in the history of our land. It belongs to the incredible tales of the dark ages. It is out of place in such a land as ours. It hardly entered into our hearts to think it *might* occur; and this has been the very cause which left our nation's ruler defenceless, and gave the assassin opportunity to execute his plans, and yet to effect his escape boldly.

Short, hasty, and unsatisfactory were the details of the blow which at first reached us,—a blow which filled every true heart with sadness, deep and solemn, while it nerved it anew to

* "J'ai parle en mon cœur, et jai dit, Voici, je me suis agrandi."—Eccl. i. 16.

a firmer purpose of loyalty and unconditional patriotism. But scanty as were the items we received, their character was such as to leave no doubt of the execution of a fearful tragedy, in the very heart of the nation's capital, among a concourse of thousands of people. Yes, it is true, — the man on whom all our eyes have been centred for the past five years, — whose labors for the public welfare were almost crushing, and, but for the happy power which he possessed of casting them off in his hours of leisure and amusement, *would* have crushed him, — the man who, calm in the consciousness of an unbending integrity, a proverbial honesty, met the gaze of the nation by a look, not of pride, but of kindly, earnest, faithful devotion to our welfare, — the man who had just received, from a grateful people emerging from the clouds of war, the laurel wreath, to wear most worthily for another term of years, —the man whose openness of heart made him accessible to all classes, so that every citizen had the consciousness that he was his personal friend, — *this* man, Abraham Lincoln, sixteenth President of the United States, fell by the hand of the assassin on the evening of April 14th of the present year.

The outline of events that presents itself is the following: Over-worn by the fatigues of office, and the importunities of selfish office-seekers, the President sought relaxation and relief in visiting places of public amusement. Relaxation of some kind was absolutely essential to a mind so overstrained. He was himself conscious of it; for while the great battle of the Wilderness was yet undecided, he remarked to a friend, who knew of his intention of going to the opera that evening, "The people will wonder, if they hear of it; but the truth is, I must have a change of some sort, or die." It may well be believed that these scenes were but little in his mind, always fertile in thoughts for the welfare of the nation in all its portions, — whether the Western frontier, the Canada coast, or the *status* of the Freedmen and the interests of Louisiana and other States about to return to their allegiance. In company with the Lieutenant-General, he had announced his intention of being thus present on the fatal evening. Circumstances called Gen. Grant away, and with his usual complaisance, unwilling to disappoint any who might wish this opportunity of seeing the leader for whom they had cast their votes, he went with his family to the place designated. At about half-past nine o'clock, during a slight pause in the entertainment, the report of a pistol was heard. It roused but little attention, many supposing it had accidentally been fired behind the scenes. In the interval of suspense a man is seen to leap upon the stage, to flourish a dagger, and exclaim, "*Sic semper tyrannis!*" then, darting away, is beyond reach, before the audience can recover from their surprise or guess his meaning. But soon cries of anguish from his family attract attention to the President, who is found dangerously wounded and insensible. Thenceforward all is confusion. The best medical help is summoned, but in vain; and in a few short hours the end of earth is reached. Meanwhile a murderous attack is made upon the Secretary of State, already in feeble health, and utterly helpless, — and which, but for the *haste* of the assassin, must have resulted fatally, if indeed it do not yet.

For this act, in all its atrocity, no *personal* motive seems possible. There was no *wrong* to be avenged, no wealth to be clutched, nothing to be gained. It does not appear (so far as I am aware) that the murderer had ever so much as spoken with the man he sought to slay. The only clew to his motives is found in his outcry, "Thus let tyrants always perish!" It was the simple act of wanton rebellion — one act — showing us its full enormity, and the spirit which actuates it.

I shall enter on no elaborate disproval of the assassin's charge. It needs to be stated only, to evince its falsity when applied to the late head of the nation. A TYRANT, we are told, is "a ruler who uses his power to oppress his subjects." Too great leniency is never the mark of such a man. But this was the most serious fault alleged against the President's personal acts, — that he was too fond of pardoning. It was his very leniency that permitted open traitors, known to be in favor of secession — and among them this very assassin — to walk the streets of Washington unharmed. This leniency has terminated in a way we shall not soon forget, — has proved itself unsafe, and full of danger: let us hope its days are numbered and finished. We have heard much of the injustice of arbitrary arrests: to-day the nation suffers because the open, avowed, and rabid treason of one man through all our conflict was suffered to be unmolested.

The name of tyrant, then, will never rest with the memory of that brave heart now low in dust. The voice of the nation in freely intrusting its affairs again so recently to one who had never abused them, effectually dispels the stigma — a shot of malice which fell harmless from the mail of honesty in which Abraham Lincoln was clad. Would that he had only been *as* invulnerable to the wound over which this day a nation weeps!

In this act, then, not dictated by any personal motive, but by the misguided theories and passions by which this rebellion has been engendered, God has permitted the nation to feel the woe and wickedness of treason. Treason has stood ready for the commission of this act whenever it should find an advocate sufficiently bold. It has aimed its blows at the innocent and unsuspecting before, in its late attempt to fire our cities. It has revealed the *merciless* character of its brutality in that ferocity which broke through the barriers which surrounded the bedside of the painful sufferer to inflict on one of the chief lights of statesmanship deep and murderous wounds. It is the same spirit which has made possible the barbarities of Southern prisons. No talents, no station, no condition, not even that of suffering, could appeal to its mercy; for it had none. No tie of honor, no tie of religion, binds it; for honor and piety were dead names in its heart long ago. If any have been disposed to treat it lightly, to be lenient towards it, look at this example, and decide *now* what it merits from you!

It is this spirit of treason and rebellion which we judge and condemn. For the unhappy criminal we have no severer doom than that which is given for a far less aggravated crime. We cannot *more* than execute the death penalty. We cannot descend to the penalties of pagan Rome or even unenlightened Europe of the middle ages. We have no rack, no wheel, no crown of red-hot iron, no quadruplicate team of horses to tear him limb from limb, as was done at Paris to Ravillac, the assassin of the King. We are above the infliction of such barbarities, which, after all, only add notoriety to the criminal, and even excite for him the sympathy of the weak-minded. We have but the death penalty, pure and simple, which even the Governor of this State must in this case approve, sanctioned as it is by Jehovah's command to Noah, the world's second great progenitor, "Whoso sheddeth man's blood, by man shall his blood be shed; for in the image of God made he man." (Gen. ix. 6.) The vengeance, hot and furious, which every one sees due, — for which this innocent blood calls, — is not ours to inflict. "Vengeance is mine; I will repay, saith the Lord." (Rom. xii. 19.) "The Lord shall reward the evil-doer according to his wickedness" — a measure which we cannot understand, but which He shall fill to its uttermost. And let us, rather than desire this work, be glad that it does *not* rest with us to perform.

In the shadow of this great sorrow — a gloom which makes the very heart heavy — a loss which seems the most severe which in the person of *one* man the nation could receive, —

there are yet considerations which we shall do well to remember, lest our hands be weak at the very time when our Government needs the greatest support both of hand and heart.

Happily, indeed, for us, God has made our dependence in this land to rest not on the life of one man, nor of *ten* men. There is no royal line made extinct; there is no usurper ready to mount *a throne* by a *coup d'état*, like that of Napoleon the Third; there is no military leader, wishing that all things may yield to arms; but in the midst of war we have chosen that a man of peaceful, not of military training, should be our Chief Magistrate; and none have been more ready in the choice than our soldiers, attached far more to native land than to any military idol. Above all, our dependence is not in man nor government, but in God. Many are the faithful hearts who have reversed the foolish action of the Israelites, who rejected God, and demanded a king, — who have long since left off to trust in princes or in man, and put *their* trust in God. They have asked him to be the Ruler of this nation, whoever might preside in its councils, — whether an administration of imbecility or one of wisdom and growing strength. And just in accordance with their faith in such a prayer will be their tranquillity, and the answer of God in accepting this election. So that, to every one who asks, "Know ye not that there is a prince and a great man fallen this day?" we may reply, Yea, I know it; hold ye your peace! "It is better to trust in the Lord than to put confidence in man. It is better to trust in the Lord than to put confidence in princes." (Ps. cxviii. 8, 9.) And here is a steadfast source of consolation, if we are willing God shall rule our nation, as well as rule in our hearts.

Let it console us, also, that this most terrible blow did not come at a time when, as a nation, our very existence was trembling in the balance. It would then have been hailed with fiendish joy by every State in rebellion. Now, however, they are so reduced that they can take no encouragement from our severe affliction. Then, also, many things were undecided, which now will cause no perplexity. Then much more power was centred in the Executive, which has at last found a faithful repository in the person of the Lieutenant-General. Much has been wisely, cautiously, *firmly* decided, which left inchoate might have involved us in far more serious economic difficulties. And when we consider the ease with which this act might before this have been perpetrated, the preservation of our ruler's life amid the tides of party passion, and against the will of hostile and disappointed politicians, may well seem to us a gift from the hand of One who is wonderful in working — though for wise reasons now showing us that *only* his power has stayed this national calamity from long ago coming upon us.

Could his removal have been anticipated by himself, it must have been a source of gratitude to our late President that he has been permitted to accomplish so much. In no portion of our nation's history has progress been so rapid as in the years of his administration. And as no one has been more worn down — not even the generals upon the battle-field — by the evils of all kinds which this rebellion has caused, so no one was more ready to welcome the signs of returning reason in those territories where anarchy has ruled, — more ready to rejoice in the victories of our arms, — to give honor to whom honor is due, — or to hail the quiet of retirement when all should have been firmly reëstablished. Sad it seems that this might not be: but though the voice of the people might call him to his place, it was powerless to preserve his life; no majority that rules or governs can say how long its chosen chief shall abide. There is the will of God above the voice of the people.

Sadly are we reminded by this event that even so death first struck down the human family, — that the first instance of his coming was one of violence, a murder, actuated by the same spirit of hatred to goodness as this base massacre. Sadly also do we remember the death which on that very day, eighteen centuries ago, the great deliverer of man suffered on the cross of Calvary, because a wicked earth could no longer endure the presence of such excellence. And now he to whom an enfranchised race have looked up to as their liberator, their earthly savior, next to Him who died for all mankind, has also fallen. The brain that planned, the hand that wrote, the Emancipation Proclamation, are silent in death. This act of freedom was never the thought of a despot, but of a wise lover of liberty; and in the beneficent results which it has already produced, he might well have rested satisfied, had this one work been the sole result of his life-long labors and his public administration. For so long as the world shall last shall the name of Abraham Lincoln be dear to a people who remember their two hundred and fifty years of bondage in a land of liberty, and whose hand it was struck off from them their fetters, and whose voice it was proclaimed them free.

Personally — and our President was so eminently a man of the people, so genial, so approachable, so social, and kind toward the afflicted and needy, that we all seem to have lost a personal friend, whether we have met him or not — personally, it is a matter over which every one will feel consolation, that, in view of his sudden death, we have the most acceptable assurance of his Christian preparation. It is not often, even in this Christian nation, that our rulers are Christian men. A lack of courage, and a most fierce opposition around them, combine to frighten such away from the toils of political life. Many there are, who, like our own Webster, sacrifice their once firm hold on heaven to gain some delusive earthly popularity or advantage. Many, like Jackson and Clay, hide their candle carefully under a bushel, suffering only a flicker of its rays to light up their death-bed. But such was not the case with him. I am relating nothing new when I call to mind his testimony of a change, of which, since he had been elevated to his office, he had been the subject. We all remember the unusual request with which he left his Western home. And yet many a man may desire, as he did, the prayers of Christians, without himself being one. His religious experience has been placed on record, and in his own words. A man, a few months since, who had some business with him, in closing, said to him plainly, "Before I left my home an aged neighbor said to me, 'You are going to Washington; you will see President Lincoln. Now I want to ask you to ask him one question for me. Ask him if he is a Christian — if he loves Jesus.' And this question, sir, I would earnestly and affectionately now make you." The President was touched to the heart, buried his head in his handkerchief a few moments, and wept. He then said, "I will answer it. When I left home to take this place, I requested my countrymen to pray for me; but I was not a Christian then. When my son died — the severest trial of my life — I was not a Christian. But when I went to Gettysburg, and looked upon the graves of our dead heroes who had fallen in defence of their country, I then and there consecrated myself to Christ. I DO LOVE JESUS." Noble profession of faith! Shall we doubt that Christ failed to recognize the allegiance of that great heart?

Nor is a practice conformable to this confession to be sought for vainly. Rev. Mr. Adams, a clergyman of Philadelphia, stated in his discourse on last Thanksgiving Day, that, having an appointment to meet the President at five o'clock in the morning, he went some fifteen minutes before that hour. While waiting in the ante-room he heard a voice near by, and asked the servant,

"Who is talking in the next room?" "It is the President, sir." "Is there anybody with him?" "No, sir: he is reading the Bible." "Is that his habit so early in the morning?" "Yes, sir: he spends every morning, from four o'clock to five, in reading the Scriptures and praying."

These testimonies are dear to the heart of a Christian nation, called in a moment to bewail the loss of its most cherished son.

So also are those manly traits of character, that frankness which seemed to delight in saying, as in his letter to Sherman, "You were right, and I was wrong," — a greatness of soul unreached by any in his station before, — that tenderness of heart which, passing the cold, dry, dreary statistics of the Military Department over, seized upon the fact that one poor woman had sent five sons to fight for freedom and lost them all, — and sent to her those words of sympathy which are more than gold, which are mint-drops of the heart.* So is that practical wisdom dear, likewise, which aimed not to teach more advanced centuries so much as to be sure that he brought up his own to the highest attainable degree.

These qualities have been well commemorated in these lines of Bryant, read on the occasion of the reception of his remains in New York City:

* PRESIDENT LINCOLN'S SYMPATHY. The following letter from the President of the United States, Nov. 21, 1864, was received by Mrs. Bixby, a poor widow in Boston: "Dear Madam, — I have been shown in the files of the War Department a statement of the Adjutant-General of Massachusetts, that you are the mother of five sons who have died gloriously on the field of battle. I feel how weak and fruitless must be any words of mine which should attempt to beguile you from the grief of a loss so overwhelming. But I cannot refrain from tendering to you the consolation that may be found in the thanks of the Republic they have died to save. I pray that our heavenly Father may assuage the anguish of your bereavement, and leave you only the cherished memory of the loved and lost, and the solemn pride that must be yours to have laid so costly a sacrifice upon the altar of freedom."

"O slow to smite, and swift to spare!
  Gentle and merciful and just!
Who in the fear of God didst bear
  The sword of power—a nation's trust—

"In sorrow by thy bier we stand,
  Amid the awe that hushes all,
And speak the anguish of a land
  That shook with horror at thy fall.

"Thy task is done: the bond are free:
  We bear thee to an honored grave,
Whose proudest monument shall be
  The broken fetters of the slave.

"Pure was thy life—its bloody close
  Hath placed thee with the sons of light
Among the noble host of those
  Who perished in the cause of Right."

But he is fallen this day—and that, too, by the way we least of all should have desired. Was, then, this new crime needed to unite ALL hearts in their hatred of that spirit of treason which inspired it? Were *other* victims also needed to show that it was the fruit of no personal animosity? And shall not the advocates of this accursed sedition and conspiracy be held to strict account for their deeds? In their mad blindness they have stricken down the man who would most have given them leniency and favor. Their *best* advocate has died. None remains who could so eloquently plead for mercy to a misled people as the tongue now silent. And in that silence all hearts hear with acquiescence the demand, Let justice *now* be done. Let all weakness be thrown away—and they that have taken and drawn the treacherous sword of cruelty—let them perish by the sword! And all people shall say Amen!

My hearers, one lesson should be taught us as we evermore think of this occurrence. The person of our rulers is entitled to respect and protection. Senseless and loud would have been the outcry had this been provided by our late ruler by an adequate body-guard. But that spirit which refused him this protection is not guiltless of his death. And if the *sorrow* of the nation shall provide a guarantee against the possibility of such an awful ocurrence again — just as in future a standing army must maintain the nation's *power* to punish — and if a suitable degree of reverence for those in whom the hopes of the nation are centred is maintained — then will not this evil and bitter thing be without fruit of good.

Finally, let us, while we remember that a prince and a great man is this day fallen — while we sorrow and detest the crime, and the deadly spirit of rebellion whence it sprung — let us still leave thoughts of vengeance to God. Nothing that man can do is adequate. Nor has God put upon man to execute full vengeance on his brother. Human justice is fulfilled when our horror of the crime and approval of the righteous penalty is made known. This is but earthly justice, imperfect both in *degree* and in *duration*. The Lord shall reward the doers of evil according to their wickedness — and it is his assurance their damnation slumbereth not!

But while men die, God lives on. He has not intended to save this nation by men. One by one, as we have leaned on rulers and commanders, He has taken them away. He will save us — of that we are sure — but it will be by his *own* hand — by the power of feeble and despised instruments it may be — yet so that we shall know the blessing is altogether *his* work. Let us unite to ask that a double portion of those excellences which especially endeared to us our late President may rest on the head of his successor: may the prayers of the nation be offered for him; and may the hand of every man be strong in the Lord to execute justice, to stand by the powers that be, and every heart invoke the protection of the Great Ruler, whose days and whose wisdom shall never know end nor decline.

www.ingramcontent.com/pod-product-compliance
Lightning Source LLC
LaVergne TN
LVHW020636110826
845149LV00004B/1234
9781418190989